Vikings

Stephanie Turnbull

Designed by Laura Parker and Hanri Van Wyk

Illustrated by Adam Larkum

Viking consultant: Dr. Richard Hall, York Archaeological Trust
Reading consultant: Alison Kelly, Roehampton University

Contents

Viking life

The Vikings were people who lived in Denmark, Norway and Sweden more than a thousand years ago.

Most Vikings lived on small farms in the countryside.

3

Different Vikings

The richest Vikings were kings and jarls, and the poorest people were thralls. Most ordinary Vikings were farmers.

Kings ruled over large areas of land called kingdoms.

Jarls were important leaders who owned lots of land.

Some ordinary Vikings worked as fishermen or traders.

Thralls were slaves who had to work for richer Vikings.

All Viking men except thralls trained to fight as warriors.

This statue shows a jarl ready to go into battle.

Many Vikings had nicknames, such as Thorkell the Tall and Eric Bloodaxe.

At home

Viking families lived in wooden or stone buildings called longhouses. There was one big room inside.

The walls of this longhouse have been removed so you can see inside.

Clothes, tools and weapons were stored in big chests or hung up on pegs.

A fire was used for cooking food and heating the room.

At one end of the longhouse was a stable for animals.

People slept on benches around the sides of the room.

Toilets were holes dug outside, often in small huts.

A trip to town

There were a few big Viking towns where people went to buy and sell goods.

Traders sold silk, spices and glass from faraway lands.

Blacksmiths shaped hot metal into tools and weapons.

People walked on paths made out of wooden planks.

8

Towns were noisy, crowded places, with animals everywhere.

People often paid for goods with coins like these, or pieces of silver from bracelets and rings.

What to wear

Vikings wore thick clothes that kept them warm when it was very cold.

Women and girls had long dresses made of wool.

A shorter dress went on top, held in place with two brooches.

Men and boys wore leggings, tunics and leather belts.

Everyone had leather shoes and cloaks of wool or fur.

These metal brooches were probably used by a Viking woman to fasten the shoulder straps of her dress.

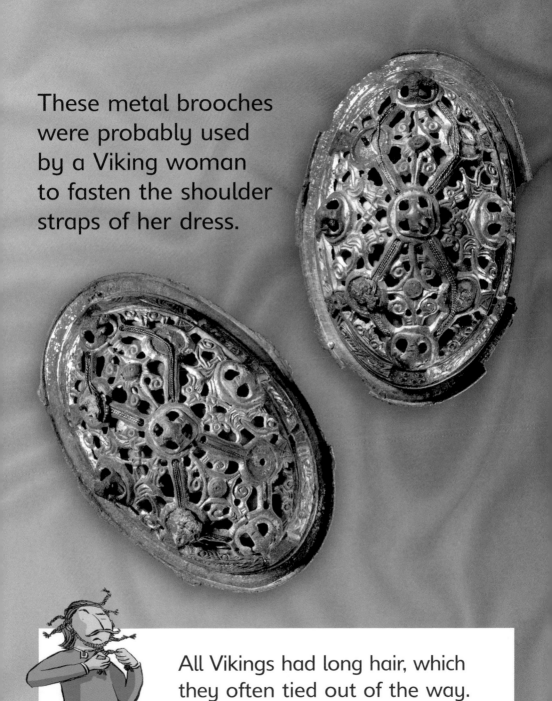

All Vikings had long hair, which they often tied out of the way.

Gods and goddesses

Vikings believed that a rainbow bridge led to a world above them called Asgard. Many gods and goddesses lived there.

This painting is about 300 years old. It shows Heimdall, a god who guarded the rainbow bridge.

Vikings thought that a giant snake circled the human world.

Odin, the king of the gods, rode an eight-legged horse.

Freya, the goddess of love, could turn herself into a falcon.

Thor was the god of thunder. He carried a magic hammer.

Loki was half-god and half-giant. He played cruel tricks on the gods.

At a feast

Vikings loved having feasts to celebrate weddings, winning wars and other events.

Thralls cooked lots of food. They roasted meat and fish over a fire and made stews.

Guests sat at long wooden tables to eat. They drank out of hollow cows' horns.

Musicians played and poets called skalds told exciting stories of battles and heroes.

There was no sugar in Viking times, but food was sweetened with honey instead.

These wooden bowls and spoons were once used by Vikings. Now they are old and cracked.

Fun and games

Vikings spent their free time playing games, repairing weapons and making beautiful things.

Some people made lucky charms like this one. It shows Thor holding his magic hammer.

Many Vikings enjoyed skiing and skating in the winter.

Sometimes men had wrestling contests or sword fights.

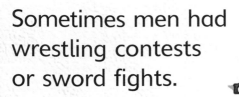

They showed off their strength by lifting huge rocks.

Vikings also enjoyed hunting with spears and arrows.

Viking boats

The Vikings were good sailors, and they made all kinds of boats. The biggest boats were called longships.

This modern boat has been built to look just like a Viking longship.

When Vikings sailed to war they hung their shields on the side of the boat, like this.

18

Long planks of wood were nailed together to make the bottom and sides of the boat.

A wide deck was added, as well as a mast for a big, square sail and holes for oars.

A dragon's head was often carved at the front of a longship to scare enemies.

Wild warriors

All Viking men owned weapons and were quick to use them against their enemies.

They wore thick leather or metal helmets.

This is a copy of a Viking helmet with eye holes and a nose guard.

A few extra-fierce, bloodthirsty warriors called themselves Berserks.

Vikings wore padded clothes for battles. Rich men had tunics made of metal rings.

They fought with swords, axes or spears. Swords were carried in a holder.

All fighters carried large wooden shields. Some men painted their shields.

Attack!

Many Vikings were poor, so they sometimes sailed to England and raided places there.

Vikings often attacked early in the morning, taking people by surprise.

They captured or killed anyone who got in their way.

Raiders set buildings
on fire to force out
the terrified people.

They grabbed all the money
and treasure they could find.

Exploring

Vikings began to raid towns all over Europe. Many of them found good land for farming and decided to live there.

Vikings also settled in Iceland and Greenland. They hunted fish, whales and seals to eat.

Some Vikings sailed as far as North America and tried to set up farms there.

They were often attacked by Native Americans, so they soon decided to leave.

The first person to sail
to North America was
Leif the Lucky.

Viking traders
went as far as
Asia to buy
and sell goods.

This modern tapestry shows Leif the Lucky
standing at the front of his longship.

Famous Vikings

The Vikings loved to tell thrilling stories about brave heroes from the past. Some of these stories might not be true.

Olaf was a king who drowned himself after losing a battle. The man jumping overboard in this painting may be Olaf.

Ragnar Hairy-Breeches was a terrifying king who once raided Paris.

Erik the Red was a fearless warrior and adventurer who explored Greenland.

Erik the Red's daughter Freydis was a skilled sailor who fought in battles.

Harald Hardrada was a clever leader who once dug a tunnel into an enemy castle.

A Viking funeral

Ordinary Vikings were buried in simple graves when they died, but important people had magnificent funerals.

Sometimes a person was placed in a boat with their belongings.

The boat was set on fire and everything was burned.

Vikings thought that dead warriors went to live with the gods.

Most other dead people went to an icy, dark world called Niflheim.

Sometimes Vikings marked graves with stones.

Glossary of Viking words

Here are some of the words in this book you might not know. This page tells you what they mean.

 trader - a Viking who bought and sold goods, often from other countries.

 longhouse - a large building where a Viking family lived.

 tunic - a long-sleeved top that was worn with a belt.

 skald - a poet who told Viking poems and long stories called sagas.

 longship - a long Viking boat used by warriors or explorers.

 raid - to make a surprise attack. Some Vikings raided towns and villages.

 Native Americans - the first people to live in North America.

Websites to visit

You can visit exciting websites to find out more about Vikings.

To visit these websites, go to the Usborne Quicklinks Website at **www.usborne-quicklinks.com** Read the internet safety guidelines, and then type the keywords "**beginners vikings**".

The websites are regularly reviewed and the links in Usborne Quicklinks are updated. However, Usborne Publishing is not responsible, and does not accept liability, for the content or availability of any website other than its own. We recommend that children are supervised while on the internet.

This dragon's head carving was found in a Viking ship.

Index

Acknowledgements

Photographic manipulation by Nick Wakeford

Photo credits

The publishers are grateful to the following for permission to reproduce material:
Jon Arnold Images/Alamy 28-29; © **The Bridgeman Art Library** 12 (Arni Magnusson Institute), 26 (Private Collection); © **Werner Forman/Corbis** 9, 16, 31; © **The Jamestown-Yorktown Foundation/The Bridgeman Art Library** 25; © **Kai Gjessing, http://Mjosen-lange.no** 18; © **Macduff Everton/Corbis** 5; © **Medieval Reproductions** 20; © **The Trustees of the British Museum** 11; © **Adam Woolfitt/Corbis** 1; © **York Archaeological Trust** 15

Every effort has been made to trace and acknowledge ownership of copyright. If any rights have been omitted, the publishers offer to rectify this in any subsequent editions following notification.

Sun, moon and stars

Farm animals

Elizabeth I

RUBBISH AND RECYCLING

Dogs

Horses and ponies

Spiders

Planes

Ancient Greeks

Cats

VOLCANOES

DINOSAURS

Your Body

Armour

Sharks

Celts

Vikings

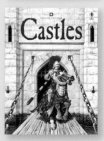
Castles

How flowers grow

Digging up the past

Living in space

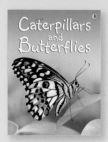
Caterpillars and Butterflies

Ballet

Pirates

Egyptians

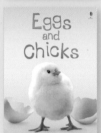
Eggs and Chicks

Romans

Weather

Tadpoles and frogs

Why do we eat?

Under the sea

Bears

Aztecs

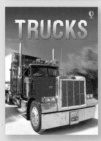
TRUCKS

Night Animals

Firefighters

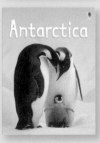
Antarctica

Bugs

COWBOYS

Planet Earth